H Caregiving
BK 4600

P9-ASJ-500

A Spirituality of Caregiving

Henri J. M. Nouwen

John S. Mogabgab, *Series Editor*

UPPER
ROOM BOOKS®

NASHVILLE

THE HENRI NOUWEN SPIRITUALITY SERIES™
A Spirituality of Caregiving
Copyright © 2011 The Henri Nouwen Legacy Trust.
All rights reserved.

No part of this book may be reproduced in any manner whatsoever without written permission of the publisher and The Henri Nouwen Legacy Trust except in brief quotations embodied in critical articles or reviews. For information, write Upper Room Books, 1908 Grand Avenue, Nashville, TN 37212.

The Upper Room website: www.upperroom.org.
The Henri Nouwen Society website: www.HenriNouwen.org

UPPER ROOM®, UPPER ROOM BOOKS®, and design logos are trademarks owned by The Upper Room®, a ministry of GBOD®, Nashville, Tennessee. All rights reserved.

Unless otherwise indicated, Scripture quotations are from *The New Jerusalem Bible*, copyright © 1985 by Darton, Longman & Todd, Ltd. and Doubleday, a division of Random House, Inc. Reprinted by permission.

Scripture quotations designated JB are taken from *The Jerusalem Bible*, copyright © 1966 by Darton, Longman & Todd, Ltd. and Doubleday, a division of Bantam Doubleday Dell Publishing Group, Inc. Reprinted by permission.

Cover and Interior Design: Sue Smith and Pearson & Co.
Cover art: Gogh, Vincent van (1889-1890). *The Siesta* (after Millet).
Réunion des Musées Nationaux / Art Resource, NY
Photo on page 70 by Mary Ellen Kronstein. Used by permission.

First printing: 2011

Library of Congress Cataloging-in-Publication Data
Nouwen, Henri J. M.
    A spirituality of caregiving / by Henri J. M. Nouwen.
        p. cm. — (The Henri Nouwen spirituality series)
    Includes bibliographical references (p.   ).
    ISBN 978-0-8358-1045-6
    1. Caring—Religious aspects—Christianity. 2. Caregivers—Religious life. I. Title.
    BV4910.9.N68 2011
    248.8'8—dc22

                                                                    2011002345

Printed in the United States of America

CONTENTS

About the Henri Nouwen Spirituality Series *iv*

Preface *v*

Acknowledgments *xi*

The Treasure 15

The Call 18

The Practice 28

The Challenge 45

The Disciplines 58

The Blessing 64

Notes 68

Henri J. M. Nouwen's Works Cited 69

About Henri J. M. Nouwen 70

ABOUT THE HENRI NOUWEN SPIRITUALITY SERIES

HENRI NOUWEN sought the center of things. Never content to observe life from the sidelines, his approach to new experiences and relationships was full throttle. He looked at the world with the enthusiastic anticipation of a child, convinced that right in the midst of life he would find the God who loves us without conditions. Helping us recognize this God in the very fabric of our lives was the enduring passion of Henri's life and ministry.

The Henri Nouwen Spirituality Series embodies Henri's legacy of compassionate engagement with contemporary issues and concerns. Developed through a partnership between the Henri Nouwen Society and Upper Room Ministries, the Series offers fresh presentations of themes close to Henri's heart. We hope each volume will help you discover that in your daily round God is closer than you think.

HENRI NOUWEN was a man of feeling. He knew the desire to respond, to soothe, to comfort, and to console. Perhaps that is why, from a very early age, he wanted to be a nurturer—a pastor, a friend, a brother, a teacher, and a writer. I suspect that as a young man he carried high expectations of self-giving and self-fulfillment that were mostly realized in the early stages of his professional life in the universities. In his passion to offer students a formation for life, he engaged them in creative prayer and dialogue and invited them to meet together with him outside of class times for community and conversation. Besides being their professor he became their friend and brother.

As time went on, perhaps because of being too alone, of being criticized by other faculty, of being overextended, and of finding himself caught in a dysfunctional system, Henri experienced failure in friendship, severe isolation, fatigue, irritability, and resentment. He gradually became conscious that his energies for nurturing were fading and his self-giving was more and more tainted with unresolved anger and inner conflicts.

Henri had the opportunity to take a seven-month sabbatical in a Trappist monastery in order to stop and look honestly at his questions. He was wise enough to know that there was nothing wrong with his desire to be a caregiver. He was also humble enough to speak candidly of his cynicism and to receive feedback from wise friends. And he was courageous enough to address what he had to change within himself so that his true human longing to care could again become life-giving and hopeful.

Over the next few years, by trial and error, Henri made some radical life changes without relinquishing his primal desire to care. Having finally settled at L'Arche Daybreak, he was ready to become responsible for community member Adam's care, although he felt profoundly inadequate. Daybreak folk remember those days after Henri's arrival and how he cringed at the community's invitation to become Adam's caregiver. At the beginning it was so challenging for him that he begged to be responsible for someone else. Besides other disabilities, Adam was unable to speak; so Henri had great anxiety about making Adam's bath a "together" time and seeing that dressing Adam and feeding him were opportunities to "get to know Adam."

A man of many words, Henri relied on normal conversation in relationships. Without this chatty give-and-take, Henri needed constant reminders to see his time with Adam less as time to complete the necessary tasks at hand and more to find a different way to communicate with Adam and thus to "be together." Gradually, very gradually, Adam became a friend who took a special place in Henri's heart and gave Henri the clarity to express his spirituality of caregiving. Henri's story, told in this book, is enlightening: "Adam became my friend, my teacher, and my guide."

But shouldn't this be Adam talking? Usually it's the fragile patient who is so grateful for a good caregiver; but in this instance the so-called stronger of the two, the caregiver, is the recipient of an invaluable gift from the so-called "non-functional" one!

This relationship of mutuality between two people brought together because of the fragility of one and the strength of the other, so routinely beautiful and yet so often stressful, is the heart of Henri's spirituality of caregiving. From his life experience as a nurturer he articulates the need for a relationship that we all know is foundational but may have forgotten because of being overextended ourselves. We may have been too alone, deeply fatigued, and discouraged, or part of a dysfunctional health care system.

Henri's spirituality of caregiving is one of encouragement for us to try another way as caregivers. He knew from personal experience how caregivers squelch their negative emotions and anxieties and plow ahead to fulfill the inescapable and unending tasks of daily caregiving without making time for the vital human exchange. He experienced the build-up of cold anger, very mixed emotions, guilt, and the heart-cry for recognition, support, and relief. And he also connected to the desperate feelings of inadequacy caregivers experience as they struggle to find time and energy to creatively steer a course towards more fulfilling and life-giving goals.

Henri's gentle challenges arise from his compassion and from his longing for us to find the courage to reopen our hearts and reclaim our truest human aspirations. His suggestions about how to take time to "be with" another person in need are meant to encourage us to stay the course, to step through the pain of difficult exchanges, and to believe in something we cannot see, hear, or touch but that we know to be vital and true.

So, as we read this book, perhaps we will give Henri permission to be *our* caregiver for a few moments. Perhaps for a brief period of time we will allow ourselves to feel that someone really does understand, that someone really does care and wants to become our friend, our teacher, and our guide.

Here is one who is convinced that care-giving can fulfill the deepest aspirations of the human heart. Here is one who has gone before us and who summons us to find wisdom and courage to more fully embrace our present reality. Here is one who, from experience and from a loving heart, supports us with promising and hopeful words: "Caregiving carries within it an opportunity for inner healing, liberation, and transformation for the one being cared for and for the one who cares."

Sue Mosteller, CSJ

The Henri Nouwen Legacy Trust

ACKNOWLEDGMENTS

Henri Nouwen never wrote a book on caregiving. And yet virtually everything he wrote, preached, or taught was rich with resonances of availability to the pain embedded in human existence. Faced, therefore, with an embarrassment of riches, Sue Mosteller and Judith Leckie have done us a great service by sifting through Henri's published works and archival papers to compile this statement of his thoughts on caregiving. As Henri's colleague at L'Arche Daybreak and a trustee of his literary estate, Sue brought to the project a penetrating understanding of the man and a thorough knowledge of his work. Judith helped bring the text to maturity through her enthusiasm for the task and sensitivity to the theme. A prodigious amount of their time, effort, and prayer has been poured lovingly into the preparation of the manuscript.

As with *A Spirituality of Fundraising*, the first volume in the Henri Nouwen Spirituality

Series, Resa Pearson and Elaine Go of Pearson and Company in Santa Clara, California, have devoted many hours to conceiving and refining the design elements of the book. Their approach has embodied the attentiveness, skill, and commitment that characterize true caregiving. Mike Walsh, executive director of the Henri Nouwen Society, has ably managed the Society's partnership with Upper Room Ministries. Sue Mosteller, Nathan Ball, Robert Ellsberg, and Kathryn Smith of The Henri Nouwen Legacy Trust have shown sustained interest in and support for the development of the series. Gabrielle Earnshaw, archivist of the Henri Nouwen Archives at the University of St. Michael's College in Toronto, has made work on this project in the Archives both productive and delightful. Sister Kathleen Flood, OP, helped identify the excerpts from Henri's other writings that appear throughout this volume.

Finally, special thanks are due to my colleagues at Upper Room Ministries. With characteristic attention to detail, Eli Fisher, Rita Collett, and Nanci Lamar ushered the manuscript through the final stages of production. And Robin Pippin, editorial director of Upper Room Books, has unstintingly shared her vision, wisdom, and good humor all along the way.

John S. Mogabgab

Series Editor

Be compassionate
just as your Father is
compassionate.
(Luke 6:36)

The Treasure

Being a Christian
is not a solitary affair.

—Behold the Beauty of the Lord

WHAT IS *care*? The word finds its origin in the word *kara*, which means to lament, to mourn, to participate in suffering, to share in pain. To care is to cry out with those who are ill, confused, lonely, isolated, and forgotten, and to recognize their pains in our own heart. To care is to enter into the world of those who are broken and powerless and to establish there a fellowship of the weak. To care is to be present to those who suffer, and to stay present, even when nothing can be done to change their situation.

To care is the most human of all human gestures. It is a gesture that comes forth from a courageous confession of our common need for one another and the grace of a compassion that binds us together with brothers and sisters like ourselves, who share with us the wonderful and painful journey of life.

In the very act of caring for another, you and I possess a great treasure. One of the great riches of caregiving is that it embraces something more than simply a focus on cure. Caregiving carries within it an opportunity for inner healing, liberation, and transformation for the one being cared for and for the one who cares. And because we who offer care and we who receive care are both strong and vulnerable, though in different ways, our coming together in a caregiving relationship is an occasion to open ourselves to receive an unexpected gift.

Therefore, I hope that this book will offer inspiration for those caring for people who are physically, emotionally, or psychologically unable to function fully on their own and who live in hospitals, institutions, nursing homes, or private residences. Many of us know from experience how hard it is to simply be a caregiver. At the same time, we may need to be reminded of how hard it is to be cared for. It isn't easy either way! But from the challenge of caregiving I truly believe it is possible to experience a more loving, mutual, and respectful relationship among us all—a spiritual bonding that carries new possibilities for mutual fulfillment and inner healing.

The Call

My true call is to look the
suffering Jesus in the eyes
and not be crushed by his
pain, but to receive it in my
heart and let it bear the fruit
of compassion.

—*Walk With Jesus*

COMPASSION AND CAREGIVING

In scripture, Jesus tells the apostles: "You are my friends, if you do what I command you" (John 15:14). And his command is: "Be compassionate just as your Father is compassionate" (Luke 6:36).

Compassion is hard because it requires the inner disposition to go with others to the place where they are weak, vulnerable, lonely, and broken. But this is not our spontaneous response to suffering. What we desire most is to do away with suffering by fleeing from it or finding a quick cure for it.[1]

Yet perhaps our greatest gift is our ability to enter into solidarity with those who suffer. Compassion can never coexist with judgment because judgment creates distance and distinction, which prevents us from really being with the other.[2]

When I reflect on my own life, I realize that the moments of greatest comfort and consolation were moments when someone said, "I cannot take your pain away, I cannot offer you a solution to your problem, but I can promise you that I won't leave you alone and will hold onto you as long and as well as I can." There is much grief and pain in our lives, but what a blessing it is when we do not have to live our grief and pain alone. That is the gift of compassion.[3]

SHIFTING PRIORITIES

Let me tell you about one life-changing care experience of my own. It happened when I was fifty-four years old, engaged full time in caring for others as pastor, priest, professor, and writer. I had just made a significant move from teaching at Harvard University to living with and pastoring people with disabilities and their assistants in the L'Arche Daybreak community in Canada.

Upon my arrival at Daybreak in August 1986 I met Adam for the first time. Although a very precious and gentle man, Adam was the most severely disabled person in our community at the time. I was soon asked to help Adam in the morning to get ready for his day. Helping Adam meant waking him up at 7:00 a.m.; bathing and shaving him; choosing his clothing and dressing him; combing his hair; walking him to the kitchen where I prepared his breakfast; sitting with him and supporting him to eat and drink; brushing his teeth; putting on his coat, gloves, and cap; helping him into his wheelchair; and wheeling him to his Day Program a few hundred yards away.

I was aghast! I simply didn't think I could do this. "What if he falls? How do I support him as he walks? What if I hurt him and he cannot tell me? What if he has a seizure? I do not even know how to dress him! So many things can go wrong. Besides, I don't even know the man. I'm not a nurse. I have no training in this kind of thing!" Some of these many objections I voiced; most of them I just thought. But the answer was clear, firm, and reassuring: "You can do it. First of all we will help you and give you plenty of time until you feel comfortable. When you feel ready you can do it all alone. Even then, you have only to call us when you have a question. It will take awhile, but you will catch on. You'll learn the routine, and you will get to know Adam and he will get to know you." [4]

In those early days, I saw Adam as someone who was *very* different from me. I did not have any expectation of developing a relationship with him because Adam was unable to speak. I worried constantly. And I kept asking myself and others, "Why have you asked me to do this? Why should I, the least capable of all the people in the house, be asked to take care of Adam and not of someone whose needs are a bit less?" The answer was always the same: "So you can get to know Adam." Now that was a puzzle for me. Adam often looked at me and followed me with his eyes, but he did not speak or respond to anything I asked him. Adam didn't smile when I did something well or protest when I made a mistake. I wondered if he even recognized me. How would I get to know him?

By concentrating on doing the right thing and making as few mistakes as possible, I finally learned the routine. I began to gain confidence in myself during the two hours I spent with Adam each day. Gradually, very gradually, things started to change. Because I was more confident and relaxed, my mind and heart were opening for a real meeting with this man whom I had joined on life's journey. My priorities, shaped for many years by books and life in some very competitive universities, were beginning to shift. What was becoming important for me was Adam and our privileged time together when he offered himself to me in total vulnerability to be bathed, dressed, fed, and walked from place to place. I was slowly getting to know him.

I also learned that Adam could communicate! He was consistent in reminding me that he wanted me to be with him unhurriedly and gently. When I wasn't really being present to him or was being too pushy he sometimes let me know by having a seizure. I realized this was his way of saying, "Slow down, Henri! Slow down." And he certainly did slow me down. I might even have to begin all over again showering and dressing him for his day! He was clearly asking me to follow *his* rhythm and to adapt my ways to *his* needs. I found myself beginning to understand a new language—Adam's language. It didn't seem to matter to me anymore that he couldn't respond in words. We were together, growing in friendship, and I was glad to be there with him.

Eventually I found myself confiding my secrets to him, telling him about my moods, my frustrations, my easy and hard relationships, and my prayer life. What was so amazing about all this was the very gradual realization that Adam was really there for me, listening with his whole being and offering me a safe place to be. I wasn't expecting that, and though I do not express it well, it really happened.

Deep friendship is a calling forth of each other's chosenness and a mutual affirmation of being precious in God's eyes.

—Life of the Beloved

Sometimes when I was anxious, irritated, or frustrated about something that wasn't happening well enough or fast enough, Adam came to mind and seemed to call me back to the stillness at the eye of the cyclone. The tables were turning. Adam was becoming *my* teacher, taking *me* by the hand, walking with me in my confusion through the wilderness of *my* life.[5]

Adam simply lived, and by his life invited me to receive his unique gift, a gift wrapped in weakness but given for my transformation. While I tended to worry about what I did and how much I could produce, Adam was announcing to me that "being is more important than doing." While I was preoccupied with the way I was talked about or written about, Adam was quietly telling me that "God's love is more important than the praise of people." While I was concerned about my individual accomplishments, Adam was reminding me that "doing things together is more important than doing things alone." Adam couldn't produce anything, had no fame to be proud of, couldn't brag of any award or trophy. But by his very life, he was the most radical witness to the truth of our lives that I have ever encountered.[6]

This story will not reflect your experience of caregiving because it is unique to me, and each encounter with another person is unique. However, I believe that my experience with Adam, together with my whole life of ministry, has taught me what I am trying to say about our inner call to care.

Caregiving is a deeply ingrained human response to suffering. We want to ease pain, to restore calm and peace to those in need. But caregiving takes a toll. There is often a huge cost to the caregiver, and sometimes the care we give springs not from a well of love and altruism but from a bitter sea of resentful duty and obligation. It is hard to listen to others when the pains and troubles of our own lives are clamoring for attention.

But if we learn to listen to our own needs and wants, that listening can free us to learn to become truly present to the inner deep and fragile beauty of those under our care. Then even the most mundane and repetitive caregiving tasks can become a means for us to grow. With patience, with time, we can develop relationships of respect, listening, presence, and truthfulness with those we care for.

We may even form a relationship with another whom we might never have chosen to know, and both be amply enriched because of it. And as the story of my time with Adam shows, the support of loving friends and colleagues is indispensable. We need help, and we should never be afraid to ask for it and never be reluctant to claim it.

The Practice

To care one must offer one's
whole vulnerable self to
others as a source of healing.

—*Aging*

THE WAY OF COMPASSION

I am convinced that caring for others who are weak or close to death is to support them in fulfilling their deepest vocation, the vocation of becoming more and more fully what they already are: beloved daughters and beloved sons of God.

Before we are caregivers, we are beloved children of God. As we come to claim this identity, we begin to see more and more that all others in our human family are also unconditionally cherished by our loving Creator. So the perspective I want to present here is based on the words of Jesus—"Be compassionate just as your Father is compassionate" (Luke 6:36)—and is offered in the deep conviction that through compassion we grow to fullness as God's beloved children. This is not said lightly. It is said after years of ministry to others: listening, visiting, reading, writing, and being called into many—often painful—experiences. There have been moments when I considered moving away from my caring ministry to easier jobs. But each time I faced this temptation, I realized that I was doubting the value of my commitment to be a follower of Jesus. As the call to compassion slowly revealed itself to me as the center of the Christian life, the thought of moving away from ministry increasingly appeared to me to be a refusal to face directly the radical challenge of my faith. The Gospel call to be compassionate is one that goes right against the grain, that turns us completely around and requires a total conversion of heart and mind. It is indeed a radical call, a call that goes to the roots of our lives.[7] So, as caregivers let us explore some of the elements of a compassionate life, for it is here that we begin to understand those words of Jesus.

MUTUALITY AND JOY

Moving towards those who suffer and sharing their pain may seem somewhat morbid. What joy can there be in solidarity with the sick and the dying? But just look at people like Francis of Assisi, Mahatma Gandhi, and Mother Teresa.

They were far from masochistic. They all radiated joy! This is because one of the most beautiful characteristics of the compassionate life is that there is always a mutuality of giving and receiving. Anyone who has truly entered into the compassionate life will say, "I have received as much as I have given." They will express deep gratitude for the gifts received from those they came to help. Joy is the secret gift of compassion.[8] A mother still deeply grieving three years after the loss of her four-year-old son was able to say how during his yearlong illness, "It was he who throughout those awful hospital experiences buoyed me up with his incredible spirit."

The "cup of sorrows" and the "cup of joys" cannot be separated.

—Can You Drink the Cup?

DISCERNMENT AND SELF-AWARENESS

It is true that most caregivers happily point to many rewarding, sometimes even wonderful, moments in their experience of giving care. At the same time, there are also many circumstances that create hardship for those living a life of compassion.

First of all, it is so important to be aware that we caregivers have a life—a life that is more than just the service of giving care. We are people who carry responsibilities with or without life partners that include nurturing children, owning homes, shopping, cooking, doing laundry, housekeeping, maintaining friendships, repaying debts, helping extended family with aging parents or with difficult sibling relationships, as well as taking responsibility for our own personal health, development, and general well-being.

We may be professional caregivers, or we may be willing or unwilling family members caring for a handicapped or aging relative, learning on the job. Our lives are full and our daily burdens are heavy. We may be underpaid or indeed, not paid at all for our services. Perhaps we do not feel listened to or recognized as a necessary link with doctors. We can also feel marginalized from the primary health-care teams that are trying to treat the one in our care. Because of all these things, we may feel devalued. If the one we care for is a family member, we also may bear all the conflicting emotions of trying to support a loved one. On the one hand, there is the desire and willingness springing from our love for this person. On the other hand, our desire and willingness may be woven together with loneliness, resentment, guilt, and shame for unwanted thoughts and dreams of being free once more from the burden of care.

We do not have to go after crosses, but we have to take up the crosses that have been ours all along.

—Compassion

Finally, if we offer care in an institutional setting, we may feel criticized by patients and by family members alike for not caring enough. We live with the high expectations both of the patient and of those who love the patients we care for. We are asked to be physically and emotionally present, to see that the one being cared for is always comfortable and clean, and to assure that the patient has what he or she may need or want—now!

At the same time and with all our good will, we caregivers may not realize that the patient does not always see the care we offer as the gift we intend it to be. Part of the difficulty may be that we tend to assume that trust is automatically given to us by the one who needs care, which may not be the case at all. My friend Anne, who is paraplegic, said to me, "I once saw a picture of St. Vincent de Paul and below it was a quotation, 'The poor have much to forgive us.' The negotiation of the carer/cared-for relationship is a delicate one. How those who are ill manage it with so much grace is a source of wonder to me. My own vulnerabilities are not so trustingly offered."

LISTENING WITH CARE

Negotiating the relationship between we who offer care and those who receive care requires listening. To listen is to become a student of the one speaking to you. Just as teachers learn their material best by presenting it to their students, so too a troubled individual best understands his or her own story when telling it to a receptive listener.

Let's reflect for a moment on our own experience. Isn't the interested listener who really wants to know our story one of the greatest gifts in life? When we have a chance to tell our story to someone who cares, we are blessed. Because it is through the listener that we discover we have a story to tell in the first place.

When someone says, "Tell me more, I really want to know," that is when we begin to realize the uniqueness of our life and the "never-heard" quality of our story. Then we become aware of the connections between events and of the trends and patterns that have led us to this place and time. We start to take ourselves seriously enough to believe that our story constitutes a unique piece of the

> *As long as we have stories to tell to each other there is hope.*
>
> —The Living Reminder

mosaic of human existence, and to realize that we do have a real contribution to make. Ultimately, we discover that we do have a gift to be grateful for, even when that gift is a life full of distortions and conflicts.

Listening, however, is not merely a sympathetic nodding or a friendly repetition of *hmm, hmm, hmm*. Listening is a very active awareness of the coming together of two lives. When I listen, I listen not only to a story, but also with a story. It is exactly against the background of my own limited story that I discover the uniqueness of the story I am privileged to hear. It is precisely with my own articulate awareness of the piece of the living mosaic that I represent that I can be surprised, sadly or gladly, and can respond from the center of my own life.

Thus, listening is a very active and extremely alert form of caregiving. It might even be a listening with words, gestures, laughs, smiles, tears, and touch. It all depends on who is telling the story and who is receiving it. The important thing is that two lives are coming together in a healing way. It is like weaving a new pattern with two different life stories stretched out on the same loom. After a story is told and received with care, the lives of two people have become different. Two people have discovered their own unique stories, and two people have become an integral part of a new fellowship. In listening we discover that caring isn't about the difference between pain and no pain, but about the difference between pain and shared pain.

Therefore, healing means, first of all, the creation of an empty but friendly space where those who suffer can tell their story to someone who can listen with real attention.

—Reaching Out

EMPATHY AND CARE

Physical pain is debilitating and tends to consume the life, mind, and heart of the sufferer. It's difficult to be unwell. And it is even more difficult to lose independence suddenly and to become dependent on another for personal help. At least initially, it is a shock to experience this dependency in the presence of all those for whom the one who suffers may have cared in times of health and physical strength. This personal vulnerability gives rise to new emotions of confusion, fear, anger, sadness, and depression, all in addition to the shock, pain, and anxiety around whatever the physical diagnosis may be.

Important for us as caregivers to remember here is that it is embarrassing to be exposed in weakness and to need help. Having managed their own lives so easily for so long for both themselves and others, those who are ill or weak may find it humiliating to have to receive care and ask someone else to help them, especially if the one asked is already busy and occupied with important matters.

Another very real sorrow for those receiving care is that it is not easy to wait—sometimes in pain—for someone to do for them what they can no longer do for themselves. It is bad enough for them to have to feel so fragile and so scared, but worse still to have to trust someone else— someone they may not know at all and who never knew them when they were strong. It can be humiliating to allow a stranger or even a family member to enter their intimate, physical, and private space. In other words, it is miserable for them to feel that they are the powerless one in the carer/cared-for relationship.

Critically ill people may experience receiving care as a huge relief. But most people, plunged into this world of receiving care, would say it is so difficult to let go, admit to needing help, and make the long and difficult passage into accepting to be beloved while in a weakened condition. It is only with much time and with loving care that they may be able to come to a new understanding of their blessedness and to realize that there is a gift awaiting them in times of sickness. Despite

> *There is no compassion without many tears.*
>
> —The Return of the Prodigal Son

having to depend more on people who have to care for them because they are physically weak, they may experience becoming fruitful in their very weakness. For example, by gratefully receiving our care they may be revealing something to us that we didn't know about ourselves—our own gifts of beauty, tenderness, and loving service. Therefore our compassionate caring must always include empathetic awareness of the inner suffering and unique blessedness of those to whom we offer care.

ENTERING THE FELLOWSHIP OF WEAKNESS

All human relationships, be they between parents and children, husbands and wives, lovers and friends, or between members of a community, are meant to be signs of God's love for humanity as a whole and each person in particular. This is a very uncommon viewpoint, but it is the viewpoint of Jesus, who says: "You must love one another just as I have loved you. It is by your love for one another that everyone will recognize you as my disciples" (John 13:34-35). And how does Jesus love us? He says: "I have loved you just as the Father has loved me" (John 15:9). Jesus reveals to us that we are called by God to be living witnesses of God's love.[9]

One of the most tragic things about our time is that we know more than ever before about the pains and sufferings of the world and yet are less and less able to respond to them. Radio, television, and newspapers allow us to follow from hour to hour earthquakes, terrorist attacks, refugees on the move, severe hunger, and an almost ceaseless litany of human suffering. The question though is, do these highly sophisticated forms of communication lead us to greater compassion?[10] It seems very doubtful because these tragedies are too distant and usually don't really touch us. We have not even met one of those suffering people. There is no relationship between them and us. However, when we are together with someone for whom we are caring, a relationship that touches our deepest hearts becomes possible and holds the potential to support each of us in becoming more fully ourselves.

Though the relationship itself seems to be between one with power and another who is powerless, it is never simply that. Instead, it is usually a rather complex, often demanding, and sometimes painful relationship. However, as caregivers we have room to grow in self-awareness and in the way we use our power in fulfilling our aspirations to help others. Right at the heart of this deeply human exchange of caring and being cared for is the opportunity to claim more fully, with all our human strengths and vulnerabilities, our identity as beloved daughters and sons of God. This very relationship between the one who offers care and the one who receives care may be a gateway

As persons we sound through a love greater than we ourselves can grasp, a truth deeper than we ourselves can articulate, and a beauty richer than we ourselves can contain.

—Clowning in Rome

for both people to enter a whole new realm of mutual healing.

But we also have to remember that although we do our best to support people in their journey to accepting their vulnerable condition, we cannot make them do it—even though it would certainly make things easier. Nor are those who need care able to make their lives easier by trying to make their caregivers look at how they exercise power. In our relationship though, there is the opportunity for each of us to be changed for the better by working to reduce the pressures and resistances in caring and by directing our focus to be more present together in a fellowship of weakness.

Anne recounted this moment of awakening in her early experience as a paraplegic: "I remember my early days in rehab hospital. I had never been in the hospital before. I gradually realized that I was now becoming part of a vast underworld of disability and suffering—of those in hospitals and elsewhere. I remember becoming aware that a hospital was somewhat akin to imprisonment and that there was a whole family of people in the prisons of the earth with whom I now had kinship."

The Challenge

When we become aware that
we do not have to escape
our pains, but that we can
mobilize them in a common
search for life, those very
pains are transformed from
expressions of despair into
signs of hope.

—*The Wounded Healer*

CARE AND CURE

Caregiving and *curing* are distinctly different from each other. People who are sick or who have a disability often demonstrate how care and cure are different. This truth is far from obvious, however, and certainly not very acceptable in contemporary society where we are, as a culture, more occupied with cure than with care.

Being a professional, particularly in this culture, implies mastering skills to repair what is broken, restore what is destroyed, reunite what is disjoined, and heal what is ill. Doctors are considered good healers when patients who entered the hospital on stretchers leave on their own two feet. Psychologists are seen to be competent when clients feel less confused after treatment than before. Social workers are deemed capable when their interventions make a difference for the life of the community. And ministers may be judged according to the success of their programs. These perceptions of the professional caregiver, which we carry unconsciously whether we are in a caring profession or not, can cause us to link our identity more with what we *do* than who we *are*.

When our identity comes more from what we do than who we are, then we have allowed ourselves, intellectually, emotionally, and sometimes even spiritually to be defined by the many "goods" or the "bads" that our world sets before us. Praise, success, and the attention of many friends make us feel happy, self-confident, and comfortable. Criticism, setbacks, and lack of attention make us feel sad, self-doubting, and lonely. When our plans work out we are all smiles; when they fail we look downcast. I vividly remember giving a lecture for a large audience. Everyone liked it except one man, who told me that I had said a lot of nonsense. When I went home, I felt depressed! A hundred successes are nullified by a single setback. One word of criticism cancels out a hundred of commendation.

As caregivers primarily concerned with cure, we may not experience much satisfaction being with people who are chronically ill or dying.

The main reason for this is because they constantly confront us with the limitations of our power to heal, and with the undeniable reality of death. But it is exactly this confrontation that opens the way for our reawakening to the deeper meaning, the spiritual treasure, of what we are doing. In our willingness to accept that we are unable to control the inevitable, and that we ourselves will also surely die, we become liberated to be true caregivers—people who are not primarily trying to cure but rather to care in the deepest sense of that word.

Cure without care makes us preoccupied with quick changes, impatient and unwilling to share each other's burden.

—Out of Solitude

CARE AND PRESENCE

Care is a strange word. It is used in many different ways and does not always communicate the essence of care as I wish to speak of it. For example, if we hear someone say, "I will take care of that guy!" we may fear there is an attack coming. Or if we are asked, "What do you want, coffee or tea?" and we reply, "Oh, I don't care," we see a very casual attitude to the choice offered us.

But real care is not ambiguous. Real care excludes indifference and is the opposite of apathy.[11] The core meaning of care—to lament, to cry out with—is first of all to "be with" the person who is suffering. To care means therefore to hear the cry and to be connected with the pain, the confusion, the loneliness, the isolation, and the sense of being forgotten before we need to "do" something about it. And to care is also to recognize how these same laments exist in our own hearts. To care includes understanding, mourning, lamenting, and identifying with those who are vulnerable and feeling weak.

My friend Anne once told me this story: "I had to return to the rehabilitation hospital. A friend came with me to give support. While I was waiting for the nurse to complete the formalities, my tears came. Such was my disappointment at having to be there, again! I looked up—both my friend and the nurse were in tears as well. I shall never forget that—the sense of being fully understood and cared for was very profound. It ended with us having a good laugh!"

In what I have said about the difference between care and cure I do not want to say that cure as a goal is unimportant. However desirable cure is, it is also possible that cure may become violent, manipulative, and even destructive if it does not grow out of care. Care is compassion. It is claiming the truth that the other person is my brother or sister—human, mortal, and vulnerable, like me. Often we are not able to cure, but we are always able to care. When care is our first concern, cure can then be offered and received as a gift.

God becomes most present when we are most human.

—Bread for the Journey

CARE AND CONVERSION

Those who are ill, injured, or elderly can help us claim the wisdom not only that all human healers have to face death, the great mocker of all cures, but also that through the love of a caring friend we can make contact with the deepest cravings of life. This wisdom not only makes us aware of the illusion of immortality but also shows us new life whenever someone says with a word or gesture, "I see your pain. I cannot take it away, but I won't leave you alone."

Maybe our deep-seated reluctance to care comes less from our concern to bring about a cure in those for whom we care than from the realization that to cry out with those who suffer, to be present to their pains, and to show compassion for their anxieties, asks us to touch our own sufferings, pains, and anxieties.

Every step we take toward deeper self-understanding brings us closer to those with whom we share our lives.

—Our Greatest Gift

Is it not true that those who confront us with their many unanswered and unanswerable questions often raise deep apprehensions within us, since they challenge us to raise the same questions in our own lives? When someone says, "I don't know if it is worth staying alive," that person may confront us with a question we have not yet dealt with ourselves; and when someone else demonstrates fear of death, he or she may prompt us to become aware of our own hidden denial of mortality.

I am not saying that we help people by confessing that we have the same problems and pains as they have. That is not caring, that simply is commiserating. But I definitely believe that we can only care to the degree that we are in touch with our own doubts and fears, just as we can only listen to the story of others with our own story in heart and mind.

Those who ask for care invite us to listen to our own pains, to know our own wounds, and to face our own brokenness. And when those who ask for care are the elderly we are also invited to realize that all pains are acolytes of our unavoidable death. I have a feeling that even as God's beloved children we each experience a profound human sadness springing from a much repressed experience of our own mortality. It is very deep. But when we are faced with another who is elderly or terminally ill, we stand squarely in front of the certainty that death is real.

It may seem a bit gruesome to talk about facing death in our own lives. And it is not surprising in our pain- and death-avoiding world that we experience this deep-seated resistance against the recognition of our own predicament. But because we may face it in those we care for, it becomes a necessity for us to accept that this fear of death is not unique to them or to us but has been with the human family since the very beginning.

Two thousand years ago the writer of the letter to the Hebrews said that Jesus faced death to "free all those who had been held in slavery all their lives by the fear of death" (Heb. 2:15). The implication here is that to live our lives in fear of death is to be in a kind of bondage, to lack the freedom to move forward in life the way we might wish to.

Breaking through our resistances around death and dying allows true liberation to take place for the giver as well as the receiver of care. We who offer care can more fully recognize and claim our own wounds, our own need of healing, and our own mortality. At the same time, we are more able to help the people we care for face their own death with grace and peace. The great mystery of care is that when the one who is cared for and the one who cares come together in common vulnerability, then both experience a new community, both open themselves to conversion, and both experience new life as grace.

The seeds of death are at work in us, but love is stronger than death.

—Finding My Way Home

How do you and I, beloved daughters and sons of God, become more open to the world of those who are broken and powerless? How, with all we have to do, can we enter with them into a more human relationship? How do we even imagine engaging others with our hearts in authentic mutuality?

Caring as God's beloved children is making the effort to be present to, listen to, and affectionately embrace a weaker brother or sister who may have been frightened by harsh comments, examined by hostile hands, or ignored by deaf ears. We do this even when we can do nothing to change the situation. This is the crux of our challenge. Whether or not we have chosen caregiving as our profession, we do profess that caring is first of all about presence to a beloved brother or sister who at this moment feels powerless. Right here, we accept in ourselves that we are not first of all someone who takes the pain away but rather someone who is willing to share it.

CARE AND THE HORIZON OF ETERNITY

To care is to be human. To be a caregiver means to allow those for whom we care to unveil our own illusions of immortality and to claim a much wider and richer understanding of life. As long as we limit our notions about health to having a strong heart, good lungs and toned muscles, as well as a lively memory, sharp insights, and quick comprehension, we are bound to have a very restricted understanding of life as God wants us to understand it. Every time we express our faith through the words of the Apostles' Creed, we say that we believe in life everlasting. It is precisely this faith in eternal life that can radically change our vision of caregiving.

Jesus speaks repeatedly about eternal life. To Nicodemus he says, "Yes, God loved the world so much that he gave his only Son, so that everyone who believes in him may not be lost but may have eternal life" (John 3:16, JB). Finally, at the end of his life, Jesus prays to his Father saying:

"Father, the hour has come: glorify your Son so that your Son may glorify you; so that, just as you have given him power over all humanity, he may give eternal life to all those you have entrusted to him. And eternal life is this: to know you, the only true God, and Jesus Christ whom you have sent" (John 17:1-3). We are called to a life eternal and, in the long run, caregiving can only be truly life-giving if it is seen and experienced in the service of eternal life. Caregiving is bringing people into touch with their most precious self, infinitely loved and cared for, and destined for a life over which death has no power. In this sense, caregiving is a preparation for eternal life.

When my clear goal is the eternal life, that life must be reachable right now, where I am, because eternal life is life in and with God, and God is where I am here and now.

—Here and Now

The Disciplines

In solitude we discover
that our life is not a
possession to be defended,
but a gift to be shared.

—*Out of Solitude*

CREATE SACRED SPACE

It requires solitude and silence to become aware of the divine movements taking place in our lives. God does not shout, scream, or push. God is love, only love, and God's Spirit is the Spirit of love longing to relate to us and to guide us to the place where the deepest desires of our heart can be fulfilled.[12] The Spirit speaks to us in silence and repeats the words of Jesus: "Don't be afraid" (John 6:19). I believe Jesus is saying, "Try not to be afraid to let go of your need to control, and let me fulfill the deep desires of your heart. Don't be afraid to rest for a moment in the truth of your beloved-ness. I am with you. Your name is written on the palm of my hand. I have loved you with an ever-lasting love. You are mine and you belong to me."

Quite a few years ago, I had the opportunity of meeting Mother Teresa. I was struggling with many things at the time and decided to use the occasion to ask Mother Teresa's advice. As soon as we sat down I started explaining all my problems and difficulties—trying to convince her of how complicated it all was! When, after ten minutes of elaborate explanation, I finally became silent, Mother Teresa looked at me quietly and said, "Well, when you spend one hour a day adoring your Lord and never do anything which you know is wrong . . . you will be fine."[13]

You and I haven't much time with our many responsibilities, but creating a small "sacred space" somewhere in our home and giving ourselves ten minutes in the morning to be with the One who loves us so as to put the coming day into loving hands, changes the way we will live it. And returning to this sacred space for ten minutes at night to recall the day's encounters, to give thanks, to ask pardon, and to put the night into the hands of Love, changes the way we sleep. This daily relationship with the loving Source of our true identity moves us towards peacefulness and joy in our lives.

O Lord, all you ask of me is a simple "yes," a simple act of trust, so that your choices for me can bear fruit in my life.

—Heart Speaks to Heart

GATHER COMMUNITY

Many caregivers experience being too alone and exhausted because of the weight of responsibility and stress involved in offering care. We need help! But finding the time and energy to ask for help is often more than we can cope with. Where possible, let us try to make the effort. For these supportive relationships may save us from the fatigue that leads to burnout.[14] The humble acts of sharing, asking, and receiving allow family members and others to become aware of their potential to care for us! By gathering supporters around us, we provide a network of relationships for ourselves and for the person in our care. In this way, our caregiving not only leads to nurturing community but also comes forth from it!

In imitation of those in our care who grow to accept care graciously, it is helpful for us to risk allowing a few others to know us in our real experience of caregiving: our feelings of being overworked, of being ashamed of secretly willing the one we care for to either get well or die, of living with the high expectations of others or feeling marginalized by professionals, of struggling under the weight of our never-ending fatigue. This may not be easy or simple for us, but let us be open to it. We truly need one or more real friends with whom to share our own feelings of frustration, powerlessness, or anxiety. When others hear, respect, and respond to our questions with gentle, supportive, and challenging honesty, we are reminded that we don't have to have all the answers and that we are not meant to be saviors. By not feeling guilty because we need others for spiritual, emotional, and physical sustenance, we are more likely to find wisdom and balance for the long haul.

Real friends find their inner correspondence where both know the love of God. There spirit speaks to spirit and heart to heart.

—The Inner Voice of Love

Finally, and where possible, caregivers need to claim relationships beyond the life of caregiving. With the help of trustworthy supporters, we may discover again the energy gained through lunch with a friend, a silent trek alone or with another through the trees or the snow, enjoying a movie or play with a family member, or having time to delve into a best-selling novel or our favorite poetry. To be connected to the arts is to be in caring relationships for our spirits.

The Blessing

God says,
Choose the blessings!

—*Bread for the Journey*

THE PERSON in need of care is a beloved daughter or son of God. That identity is unchanged by weakness, illness, or death. When Jesus says, "Blessed are the poor" (see Luke 6:20), he is speaking not just of the poor economically but of each of us, his beloved brothers and sisters, when we experience our human fragility. That basic human weakness is never more evident than when people fall sick or face the reality of their death. Perhaps not so strangely, however, people seldom consider themselves "blessed" when weakness befalls them.

We want to help. We want to do something for people in need. We want to offer consolation to those who are in grief and alleviate the suffering of those who are in pain. There is obviously nothing wrong with that desire. It is a noble and grace-filled desire. But unless we realize that God's blessing is coming to us from those we want to serve, our help will be short-lived, and eventually we may feel burned out.

How is it possible to keep nursing the sick when they are not getting better? How can we keep consoling the dying when their deaths only bring us more grief? The answer is that they all hold a blessing, a blessing that each of us needs to receive. Caregiving is, finally, receiving God's blessing from those to whom we give care. What is the blessing? It is a glimpse of the face of God. Seeing God is what heaven is all about! We can see God in the face of Jesus, and we can see the face of Jesus in all those who need our care.

This is the mystery of the Christian life: to receive a new self, a new identity, which depends not on what we can achieve, but on what we are willing to receive.

—Compassion

We so much need a blessing.[15]

Those in need of our care are waiting to bless us.

Give, and there will
be gifts for you: a full
measure, pressed down,
shaken together, and
overflowing, will be
poured into your lap.

(Luke 6:38)

NOTES

1. *The Way of the Heart: Desert Spirituality and Contemporary Ministry* (Harper Collins, 1981), 24–25.

2. *Way of the Heart*, 26.

3. *Here and Now: Living in the Spirit* (The Crossroad Publishing Company, 1994), 105.

4. *Adam: God's Beloved* (Orbis Books, 1997), 42.

5. This section slightly adapted from *Adam,* 43–48.

6. *Adam,* 55–56.

7. This section adapted from Henri J. M. Nouwen, Donald P. McNeill, and Douglas A. Morrison, *Compassion: A Reflection on the Christian Life* (Doubleday, 1982), 7–8.

8. *Here and Now,* 102–103, 107.

9. *Here and Now,* 127.

10. Adapted from *Compassion,* 50.

11. *Out of Solitude: Three Meditations on the Christian Life* (Ave Maria Press, 1974), 33.

12. *Here and Now,* 52.

13. *Here and Now,* 88.

14. This section inspired by Michelle O'Rourke, *Befriending Death: Henri Nouwen and a Spirituality of Dying* (Orbis Books, 2009), 121.

15. *Here and Now,* 82–83.

HENRI J. M. NOUWEN'S WORKS CITED

Page 15: *Behold the Beauty of the Lord* (1987), 59.

Page 18: *Walk With Jesus* (1990), 29.

Page 24: *Life of the Beloved* (1992), 54.

Page 28: *Aging* (1974), 97.

Page 31: *Can You Drink the Cup?* (1996), 54.

Page 33: *Compassion* (1982), 73.

Page 35: *The Living Reminder* (1977), 66.

Page 37: *Reaching Out* (1975), 67.

Page 39: *The Return of the Prodigal Son* (1992), 120.

Page 42: *Clowning in Rome* (1979), 99.

Page 45: *The Wounded Healer* (1972), 93.

Page 48: *Out of Solitude* (1974), 36.

Page 50: *Bread for the Journey* (1997), October 2.

Page 51: *Our Greatest Gift* (1994), 51.

Page 55: *Finding My Way Home* (2001), 156–57.

Page 57: *Here and Now* (1994), 69.

Page 58: *Out of Solitude* (1974), 22.

Page 60: *Heart Speaks to Heart* (1989), 24.

Page 62: *The Inner Voice of Love* (1996), 80.

Page 64: *Bread for the Journey* (1997), September 8.

Page 66: *Compassion* (1982), 20–21.

ABOUT HENRI J. M. NOUWEN

Mary Ellen Kronstein

Henri Nouwen and John Mogabgab at Notre Dame in 1978

INTERNATIONALLY RENOWNED author, respected professor, and beloved pastor, Henri Nouwen wrote over forty books on the spiritual life that have inspired and comforted countless people throughout the world. Since his death in 1996, an ever-increasing number of readers, writers, and researchers are exploring his literary legacy. Henri Nouwen's works have been translated and published in more than twenty-two different languages.

Born in Nijkerk, Holland on January 24, 1932, Nouwen was ordained in 1957. Moved by his desire for a better understanding of human suffering, he went in 1964 to the United States to study in the Religion and Psychiatry Program at the Menninger Clinic. He went on to teach at the University of Notre Dame, the Pastoral Institute in Amsterdam, and the Divinity Schools of both Yale and Harvard, where his classes were among the most popular on campus.

His strong appeal as a teacher and writer had much to do with his passion to integrate all aspects of his life into a lived spirituality. Nouwen was convinced that striving for such integration is an urgent need in our culture. His writing, often autobiographical, has given readers a window into the joys and struggles of their own spiritual quest. The universal character of Nouwen's spiritual vision has crossed many boundaries and inspired a wide range of individuals: Wall Street bankers, politicians and professionals, Peruvian peasants, teachers, religious leaders, ministers and caregivers.

Nouwen traveled widely during his lifetime, lecturing on topics such as ministry and caregiving, compassion, peacemaking, suffering, solitude, community, dying, and death.

Nouwen was always searching for new images to convey the depth of the good news of the gospel message. For example, Henri met and befriended a group of trapeze artists in a traveling circus. Just prior to his sudden death, he was working on a project to use life in the circus as an image of the spiritual journey. *The Return of the Prodigal Son*, one of his classic works, marries art and spirituality in a contemporary interpretation of the ancient Gospel parable.

Henri lived the last ten years of his life with people who have developmental disabilities in a L'Arche community near Toronto, Canada.

Inspired by Henri Nouwen's conviction that one's personal relationship with God is the foundation for all other relationships, the Henri Nouwen Society exists to create opportunities and resources that support people in their desire to grow spiritually.